Music Hall

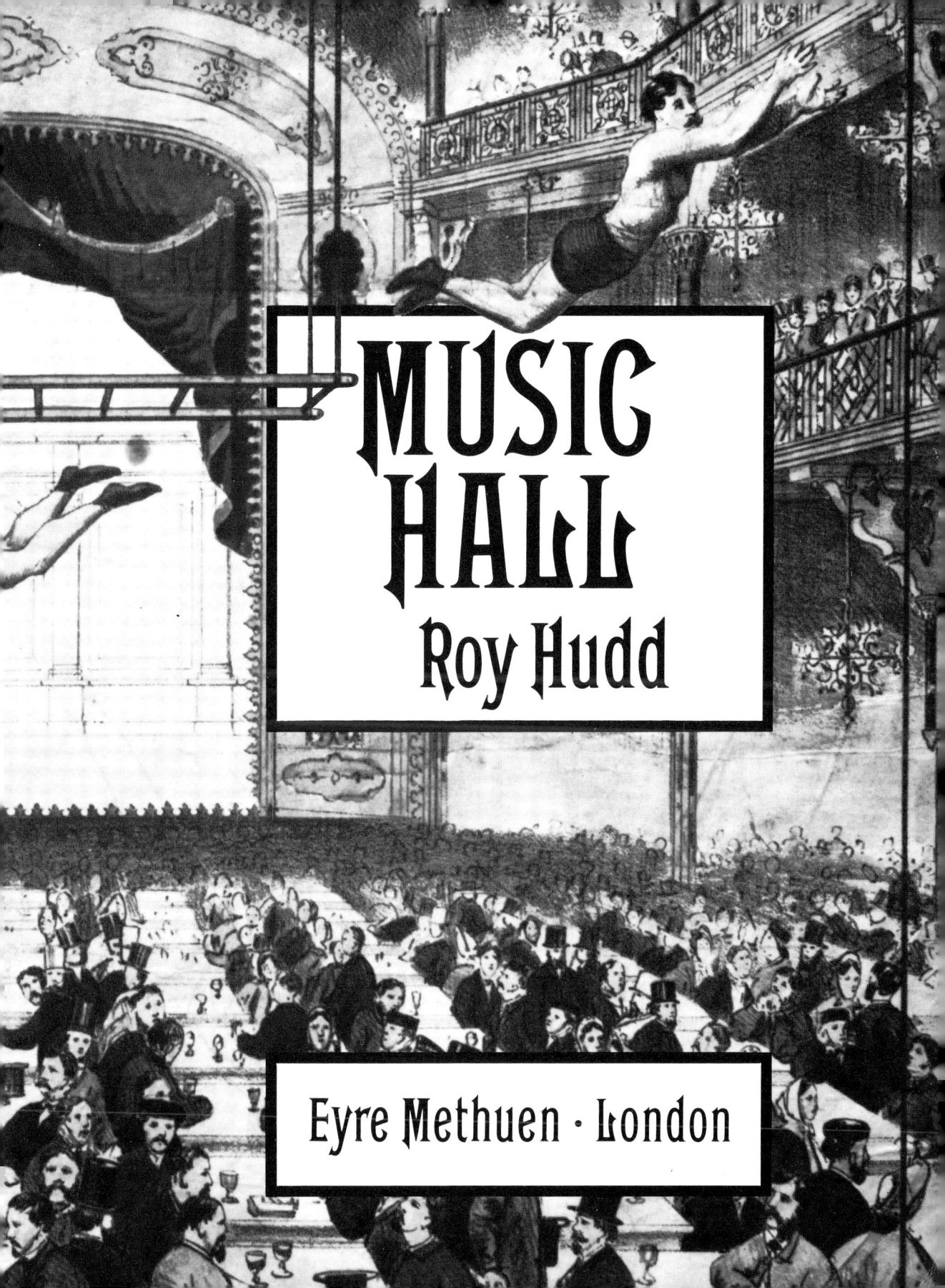

MUSIC HALL

Roy Hudd

Eyre Methuen · London

PICTUREFILE

First published 1976
by Eyre Methuen Ltd
11 New Fetter Lane, London EC4P 4EE
Copyright © 1976 Roy Hudd
Filmset by Keyspools Limited,
Golborne, Lancashire
Printed in Great Britain
by Hazell Watson & Viney Ltd.,
Aylesbury, Bucks.

ISBN 0 413 33430 9

Picture Credits

Acknowledgements and thanks for permission to reproduce pictures are due to Roy Hudd for pages 1, 13, 16, 19, 21, 23, 29, 33, 35, 36, 37, 39, 50, 51, 64, 70, 71, 74, 85, 87, 88, 91, 93, 96, 98, 100, 102, 103, 108, 110, 111, 115, 120, 121, 125 and 128—to the Radio Times Hulton Picture Library for pages 2, 3, 8, 15, 17, 18, 25, 34, 35, 41, 42, 44, 45, 46, 48, 49, 52, 53, 61, 62, 73, 77, 83, 86, 87, 91, 92, 101, 117 and 127—to Ellis Ashton for pages 4, 5, 6, 7, 20, 32, 43, 45, 47, 55, 72, 74, 75, 76, 79, 84, 89, 90, 94, 95, 97, 114, 118 and 126—to David Cheshire for pages 22, 50, 51, 54, 76, 90, 93, 97, 104, 105, 107, 109, 112 and 113—to John Freeman for pages 24, 58, 69, 80, 81, 82 and 89—to the BBC for pages 30, 31, 123, 124 and 125—to the Guildhall Library for pages 14, 15, 28 and 41—to Kent County Libraries for pages 11, 12 and 78—to the Mary Evans Picture Library for pages 10, 27 and 67—to the Press Association for pages 56, 57 and 59—to the Liverpool Record Office for pages 62, 63 and 122—to Contemporary Films for page 123—to Cleveland County Library for page 66 and to Lincolnshire County Library for page 65. The pictures on the front and back covers are reproduced by kind permission of Roy Hudd, Ellis Ashton and John Freeman.

No copyright has been wittingly infringed in any picture reproduced in this book.

Grateful thanks are due to David Cheshire for the picture research.

Introduction

An evening in a Music Hall was, until moving pictures came along, Britain's most popular night out. It was a purely British form of entertainment and, for around three quarters of a century, a highly successful one. Like all popular entertainments it grew out of a need. The huge increase in urban population during the first half of the nineteenth century needed, albeit for a few short hours, to be taken out of its humdrum existence, and amused. Music Hall amused in style. At nominal cost it seated its audience in palatial surroundings, provided drink, made them laugh and cry at their lot and sent them singing homeward.

The songs of the Music Hall are its most important contribution to our heritage. Like all good songs they reflect the lives, opinions, loves and hates of the generation they were written for. The Beatles did it in the 1960s. A folk song, to me, is a song that people remember and pass on to their children. If we British have any folk songs at all these are they. Listen to a pub or coach outing sing-song anywhere in the British Isles and you'll hear teenagers singing Music Hall songs that are often over a hundred years old.

The period when Music Hall was king is generally accepted as being from roughly around 1850 to the outbreak of the First World War. To the historian and student of sociology this period is valuable. But to the person who is interested in popular entertainment, popular entertainers and popular songs it is inescapably fascinating.

This book is a skeleton history, as well as a celebration, of the Halls. I hope you'll provide the flesh yourself. I've sprinkled lots of book titles throughout. They're books that I've enjoyed, they're packed with information, anecdotes and, best of all, they are, like Music Hall itself, entertaining. What I've tried to do is provide a sort of Music Hall primer. My whole aim is to whet your appetite, to give you just a taste of the delights that can be yours if you decide to follow up the 'teasers' I've put together.

My own interest in the subject stems from childhood. My dear Gran, who brought me up, regularly sacrificed a couple of bob from her pension to take me to the old Croydon Empire. She always used to make me rub the whitewash (collected from the stone steps we used as seats in the gallery) from the back of my shoes before we came out. "I don't want people to know we can only afford the 'Gods'". Here I saw many of the 'Veterans of Variety' and even as a boy I fell in love with their individuality, their style and their songs.

Sixteen years ago I came into show business myself. I just caught the very end of the Variety era. Some people say I hastened it! It was

sad seeing all the old theatres close and even sadder chatting to old performers who set me on fire with their stories of the good old days. I collected their anecdotes and their songs, I read what I could and spent hours rooting around in junk shops for photographs and programmes. I wanted to know more and more about the beginnings of the profession I love. The man who helped me more than any other in my quest for knowledge was Charles Chilton.

Charlie (as we all know him) is a BBC radio producer who wrote, devised and produced two series of 'Roy Hudd's Vintage Music Hall'. Charlie, whose many claims to fame include devising 'Oh What A Lovely War', is a magician. He managed to recreate, in twenty-six programmes, the whole Music Hall era. He introduced me to words and music forgotten by almost everyone. He painted, in sound, unforgettable pictures of all the things that intrigued me.

That was it, I was hooked, and here I am, trying, without Charlie's special gifts, to get you hooked too.

Of course, for me and millions of people Music Hall is still very much alive. Just go along to any of the big clubs all over the country and you'll find all the things that made Music Hall tick still working. You'll find good compères who know their audience and can handle them just like the old chairmen. You'll be able to eat and drink, join in popular songs and enjoy comedians who crack gags about contemporary life. Please give it a try.

But back to the book. I should like to thank Charlie Chilton, Lilian Aza, Don Ross, Jack Walsh, John Duncan, Ronnie Brandon, Dickie Pounds, David Cheshire, Alice Mary Barham, Tommy Dennis, Georgie Wood OBE, Raymond Mander, Joe Mitchenson and all the people who opened the wonderful world of Music Hall for yours truly.

If this book does for you what they did for me, then I've succeeded.

1. *Supper at Vauxhall Gardens* (1732–1859). An illustration by
George Cruikshank.

The earliest references to anything like Music Hall I can trace go back to the fairs of the Middle Ages. Most had platforms or booths where variety-type shows were presented.

In Shakespeare's time many playhouses occasionally dropped the legitimate drama to present variety bills in order to save their Bacon financially.

In the late seventeenth century we're getting nearer the real thing with the fair singing booths.

The popularity of the Pleasure Gardens (How many times have you seen an acrobat or juggler appearing in front of a backcloth like this?) meant open-air concerts and the building of special concert rooms where artistes from the theatres would oblige with favourite ballads.

The Pleasure Gardens, however, were fairly genteel and upper class so it was the popularity of Tavern sing songs that began to make the music hall. In the 1760s publicans would present amateur concerts of a very free-and-easy nature for their customers. The pub owners soon noticed that more people turned up to buy their booze when certain performers appeared so they began to pay the most popular. These Tavern concerts developed into The Song and Supper Rooms which sprang up all over London. The host became the chairman to introduce the performers and encourage drinking and we were nearly there.

Some great stuff on the pre Music Hall period is in *The Early Doors* by Harold Scott.

2. The type of speciality act featured in fairground booths since
the Middle Ages.

Musical Melange.

Assembly-Rooms, Margate.

FOR THE BENEFIT OF

Mr. BROADHURST

20th, 1815.

MERS.

WILLIAMS,
the King's Chap^l.
ST.

DON,

d to give his powerful assistance

begs leave to
and Public of
have the honor
nment, consisting

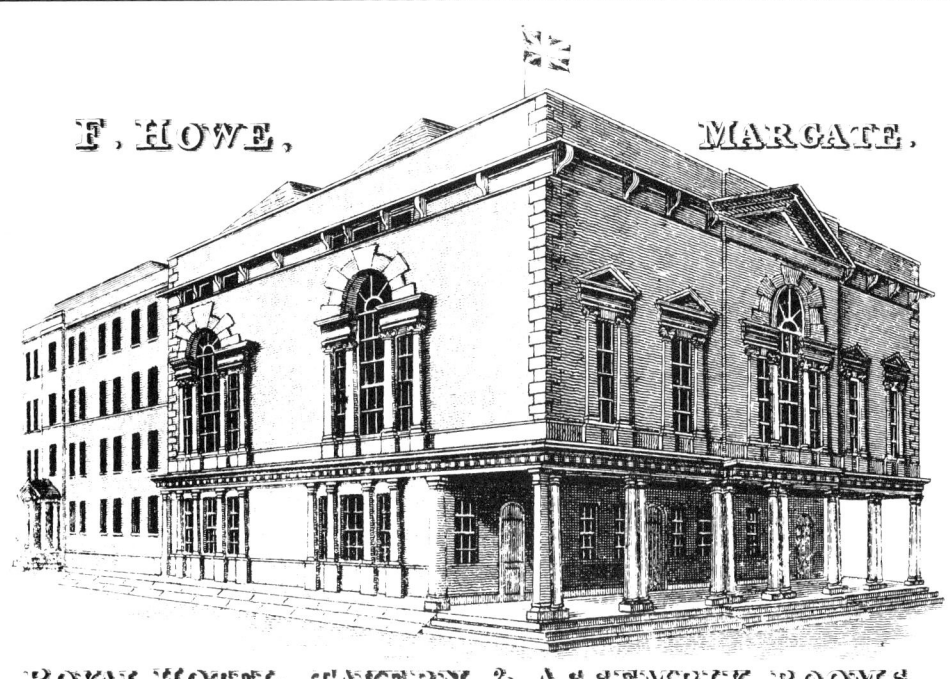

F. HOWE,   MARGATE.

ROYAL HOTEL, TAVERN & ASSEMBLY ROOMS.

ling, &c.

DENOMINATED

The MINSTRELS,

CONSISTING OF

Comic Oral Matter, Songs, Glees, &c. from the most approved Masters.

The Reading by Mr. MELVIN.

The Songs accompanied on the Grand Piano-Forte by Mr. Broadhurst.

PART I.

GLEE . . *The Red Cross Knights.*
SONG . . Mr. Incledon . . *The Isle of Britain* . . BISHOP.
SONG . . Master Williams . . *Kate Kearny.*
Song . . Mr Broadhurst . . *Fly not yet* . . IRISH MELODIES.
Mr. Incledon . . *The Bay of Biscay.*
n of Margate, Packet, Steam Boat, &c. . . Mr. Mel
Oh 'tis sweet to think . . IRISH MELODIES.
. . Miss Broadhurst.
edon . . *Blow high Blow low.*
Jessy o'Dumblaine . . SCOT'S MELODIES.
cian outwitted . . Mr. Melvin.
ncledon . . *Black ey'd Susan.*
Song . . M roadhurst . . *The Death of Abercrombie.*
GLEE . . . *Bells of St. Michael's Tower* . . . by Mr. INCLEDON, Mr. Broadhurst, and
Master Williams.

3 & 4. A rather high-tone Tavern Concert – the Assembly Rooms
(Concert Rooms) being attached to the Royal Hotel (pub). The
artistes featured are professionals from the legitimate theatre.

CANTERBURY THEATRE.

The Public are respectfully informed that

Mr. Grimaldi

having received information that his services are not required at the Theatre Royal
Covent Garden THIS EVENING, MR. DOWTON has availed himself of the opportunity,
and begs leave to announce that he will appear for

ONE NIGHT MORE.

This present TUESDAY EVENING, MAY 6, 1817,

Will be performed SHERIDAN's Popular Comedy of

THE RIVALS

OR, A TRIP TO BATH.

The Part of BOB ACRES, by MR. GRIMALDI,

As performed by him at the Theatre Royal Covent Garden.

Sir Anthony Absolute, Mr. WHARTON.   Captain Absolute, Mr. W. DOWTON.
Sir Lucius O'Trigger, Mr. HAMERTON.   Faulkland, Mr. MARSHALL.   Fag, Mr. HAMERTON, jun.
David, Mr. H. DOWTON.
Julia, Miss BARRY.   Lydia Languish, Miss LEIGH.   Lucy, Miss NEVILLE.   Mrs. Malaprop, Mrs. OWEN.

In the course of the Evening the following

COMIC SONGS,
By Mr. GRIMALDI

By Particular Desire, his popular

"TIPITYWICHET,"
Or Pantomimical Paroxysms.

THE CLOWN'S SWALLOW,
Or the Monument in Danger.

AND

"ONE OF EVERY SORT."

The whole to conclude with the Grand Serious Pantomime of

DON JUAN

Or, The LIBERTINE DESTROYED.

The Part of SCARAMOUCH, by Mr. GRIMAI

Don Juan, Mr. W. DOWTON.
Don Guzman, Mr. WHARTON.   Don Fernando, Mr. POWER.   Fisherman,
Alguazile, Mr. HAMERTON.
Sailors, Mr. H. DOWTON.   Mr. OWEN, Mr. HAMERTON, jun. &c.
Dancers, Villagers, &c.
Donna Anna, Mrs. ROBINSON.   Attendant, Miss A. LEIGH
Fishermens' Wives, Miss KENNEDY and Miss WHITAKER.   Old Woman,

Doors to be opened at Six, and begin at Seven.—Tickets and Places to be taken of Mr. HARRY,
the Dwelling-house adjoining the Theatre.

PRINTED BY B. BAINES, (Kent Herald Office,) CANTERBURY,

5. *above :* Even though Grimaldi was appearing in Sheridan's 'The
Rivals' his comic song 'hits' are featured very strongly.

6. *opposite :* Grimaldi – 'appearing in public'.

George Cruikshanks

Some interesting books on Grimaldi and pantomime: *Memoirs of Grimaldi* edited by Charles Dickens, *Grimaldi, King of Clowns* by Richard Findlater, *The Story of Pantomime* by A. E. Wilson, and *Pantomime* by Raymond Mander and Joe Mitchenson.

Joseph Grimaldi (1778–1837) 'The King of Clowns'

Not, of course, a music-hall star but someone who would have been if music halls had been around.

Joseph Grimaldi was the most famous pantomime clown of all time. Clowns to this day are called 'Joey' because of him.

The son of a famous ballet master and mime artiste he was onstage himself at the age of two. At three he was in pantomime at Drury Lane. During these early years he would often appear at both the Lane and Sadler's Wells on the same night. He became a star with his appearance in 'Mother Goose' at Covent Garden Theatre in 1806 and stayed one until his early retirement in 1828.

His appeal, apart from his amazing inventiveness, lay in his personality. 'It wasn't what he did it was the way he did it'. (How many times have we heard that said about great comedians.) He had some very popular songs—'Tippitywitchet' and 'Hot Codlins' (Toffee Apples), both of which later clowns were made to sing, by public demand.

He died crippled by overwork at the age of 58.

Aucto Splendora Resurgo.

A correct representation of the Interior of the Great Room, under the Street,

Adelphi Shades,
ADAM STREET, STRAND;

Being the only one of the kind, and allowed by all visitors, to be the greatest Novelty in London.

GENTLEMEN

Frequenting the Theatres, or otherwise, will find this a very eligible place for all Suppers and Refreshments, which are prepared at all hours with every attention to comfort and economy.

THE HARMONIC MEETINGS.

Are of a superior description and conducted upon liberal principles.

EVERY EVENING

The Vocal Talent is supported by that Son of Fun, Frolic and Whim,

Charles Sloman, the Improvisitiore,

Assisted by several Gentlemen of first rate Professional Celebrity.

JOHN REGAN,

With the utmost respect, begs to return his sincere thanks for the patronage which he has already received since entering the above establishment; and begs to inform the Public and his Friends, that he has carried into execution various improvements in every department which renders it superior to any at present existing in London.

THE ROOM has been acknowledged by all visitors to demand attention from its UNIQUE SITUATION, whilst the interior embellishments have been planned with every regard to convenience and comfort. It is the intention of the Proprietor to provide a SUCCESSION OF AMUSEMENTS, which will ensure a pleasant, social, and mental repast, whilst partaking of the more substantial comforts which the Establishment affords.

Families supplied with Bottled Stout, Fine Edinburgh Ale, Cyder and Perry. Orders executed from the Wholesale Department.

7. Interesting (*opposite*) is the billing of Charles Sloman of the Song and Supper Rooms – his appeal lay in his being able to improvise verses on any subject (rather like Lance Percival does today). He also composed a song 'The Maid of Judah' which he always sang, even though he had a bad voice. One night as he sang, 'No more shall the children of Judah sing', a customer, who'd had enough, shouted 'Well if they can't sing better than that, it's a —— good job!!

8 & 9. The cartoon shows The Cyder Cellars in full swing. No one seems to be taking a blind bit of notice of the performer! He is giving them 'The Ballad of Sam Hall', the big hit of W. G. Ross, whose powerful singing of this tale of a murderer in the condemned cell made him a star. Copies of the portrait (*top*) were sold for a shilling each. A short burst of the song will give you an idea of it's content:

  The parson he did come
  And he looked —— glum
  He can kiss my ——! ——!
  —— his eyes!
Lovely stuff!

MANNERS . AND . CVSTOMS . OF . Yᵉ . ENGLYSHE . IN . 1849.   Nᵒ 2 3.

A . CYDERE : CELLARE . DVRYNG A . COMYCK . SONGE .

KING LEAR

AND HIS DAUGHTERS QUEER.

HUGO VAMP'S

COMIC DRAMATIC

SHAKESPEREAN SCENAS.

VERSIFIED VOCALIZED & SUNG IN HIS OWN ENTERTAINMENT

BY HUGO VAMP.

SUNG ALSO BY S. COWELL, R. GLINDON & OTHERS.

LONDON: DAVIDSON, PETERS HILL, ST. PAUL'S.

E.ng. Ste. Hall.

Price 6d

10 & 11. Sam Cowell (1820–1864). A former actor (descendant of
the Kemble and Siddons families who became a music-hall star
with cockney character songs like 'Vilikens and his Dinah' and
'The Ratcatcher's Daughter'. He also told Shakespearian stories
in song parody form (*opposite*) Charles Chilton dug one of these
out and I did it on a radio show. It was still very funny. Sam
Cowell's grave can still be seen at Blandford, Dorset. One of Sam's
descendants, Barry Kemble, is the stage manager at the Winter
Gardens, Bournemouth.

12 & 13. Frederick Robson (1821–1864). 'The Great Little
Robson', an actor who first featured Sam Cowell's big hit
'Vilikens and his Dinah' in a musical and after the play in various
saloons. He suffered such a stage fright that while waiting for his
cue he would 'gnaw his arms till they bled'.

VILIKENS AND HIS DINAH,

M.ᴿ F. ROBSON, AS JIM BAGS.

SUNG BY
M.ᴿ F. ROBSON,
IN THE MUSICAL FARCE OF
THE WANDERING MINSTREL,
AS PERFORMED AT THE
ROYAL OLYMPIC THEATRE

14. The whole idea of a white man painting himself black seems hysterical to me but without it perhaps we'd have never had that magical artiste G. H. Elliott (1882–1962). I wonder what the race relations board would make of that lot!

E. W. Mackney, from a Photograph by A. Silvester

15. E. W. Mackney (1823–1909). The *Great* Mackney, one of the
first performers to 'black up' and one of the few early stars to live
to a ripe old age, for most of them worked and boozed themselves
to an early grave.

16 & 17. Here's another one! Eugene Stratton (1861–1918).
Perhaps the most famous minstrel of all. He was a fabulous soft-
shoe dancer with some great songs, including one of the greatest,
'The Lily of Laguna'. Contemporary reviews of his act send
shivers up my spine. On his dancing – 'beautiful beyond words',
'he moved like a spirit of the air'. On his singing – 'He acted the
song rather than sang it, he lived the whole thing and *was* what
the song represented him to be! Oh for a time machine!

THE LILY OF LAGUNA

Written and Composed
by

Leslie Stuart ©

Sung by

Eugene Stratton ©

W. George

Copyright.

Price 4/=

LONDON;

FRANCIS DAY & HUNTER 142 CHARING CROSS ROAD OXFORD STREET END

18 & 19. Buildings, to me, are not what Music Hall was all about.
I prefer people. But I include these views of the Canterbury Hall
(opened in 1852) because it was, debatably, the very first real
Music Hall.

The Canterbury Hall (1852–1912).

The Canterbury Hall, added to a pub, The Canterbury Arms, in 1852, is generally regarded as the first real Music Hall, in that it was especially built to house entertainment.

It's builder was Charles Morton (1819–1904), 'The Father of the Halls'. He had owned pubs and promoted simple Tavern Concerts, but, realising the potential of the Lambeth area, he took a chance and added the purpose-built, seven-hundred-seater, hall to The Canterbury Arms.

It was a tremendous success. The entertainment, at first, was of a rather highbrow nature. Classical music was heavily featured. Gounod's 'Faust' was first sung at the Canterbury and Offenbach's music gained its English popularity there. Of course the comic singers couldn't be kept out and as time passed they became the 'draws'.

Several successful halls and an art gallery were built on the original site, each one more splendid than the last. Morton, however, did not stay at The Canterbury; he sold up in 1867 and went on to a glittering career in Music Hall. He built the Oxford Music Hall on the corner of Tottenham Court Road, ran, and saved from financial disaster, many theatres including the Tivoli and the Alhambra. At the age of 74, he did the same job for the Palace Theatre, Cambridge Circus. He remained in charge of this beautiful theatre practically up to his death at 86 in 1904. He left only two thousand pounds to his family, but to us all he left Music Hall.

THE CANTERBURY.

21 & 22. Sam Collins (1827–1865) was a London chimney sweep
who became the archetype stage Irishman. He hit the big time
working for Charles Morton at the Canterbury and in 1862
opened his own hall. Collins' Music Hall remained in Islington for
a hundred years. Sam's tombstone in Kensal Rise Cemetery has
his portrait, a shillelagh and a long inscription. Do have a look.

23. The interior of Wiltons Music Hall as it is today. This very early Hall was built on to The Prince of Denmark pub by John Wilton in 1856, just four years after the Canterbury. It was the local for sailors from the London Docks and a very lively place. As well as grub and numerous bars it boasted a private entrance to the brothel next door. All this and turns too! Wiltons remained a Music Hall until 1888 when two old ladies turned it into a Wesleyan chapel.

The Hall was rediscovered after the Second World War, standing alone amid the bomb damage, exactly as it was when built.

After pressure from all sorts of nice people the GLC put a preservation order on it. What next?

I've done a couple of television shows from there and it's a beautiful hall to work in. You can almost see Sam Cowell, Sam Collins, and E. W. Mackney on that tiny stage. You can have a look at the place (if you're lucky enough to catch the caretaker in): it's situated just off Wellclose Square in Graces Alley, quite close to the Tower of London. Try and see it.

Harry Clifton (1832–1872)

Another star who successfully travelled from the Song and Supper Rooms to the early Music Halls. He has always fascinated me as so many of his songs (which he wrote himself, even though he knocked off most of the tunes) are pompous and full of advice. Here are just some of the titles:

'Always put your shoulder to the wheel'
'A motto for every man'
'Paddle your own canoe'
'Act on the Square'
'Work Boys Work'—this one goes on

> Work Boys work and be contented
> As long as you've enough to buy a meal
> For that man, you may rely
> Will be wealthy by and by
> If he'll only put his shoulder to the wheel

Take that the TUC! Need I tell you his songs were very popular in the Victorian parlour. They did all have rattling good tunes though and I can't help liking him for a trio of delightful songs he wrote,
'Shelling Green Peas'
'The Dark Girl Dressed in Blue'
and my very favourite song of all
'Pretty Little Polly Perkins of Paddington Green'.

The tune is a lovely traditional air, it has a very good story and some beautiful words—here's just the chorus:

> Oh—she—was—as—
> Beautiful as a butterfly
> And as proud as a Queen
> Was Pretty Little Polly Perkins
> of Paddington Green!

Remember it now?

WATER-CRESSES.

And she promised for to marry me
Upon the first of May
When she left me
With a bunch of Water Cresses.

WRITTEN COMPOSED & SUNG WITH UNBOUNDED APPLAUSE BY

HARRY CLIFTON.

Pnt. Sta. Hall.   Pr 2/6

LONDON, HOPWOOD & CREW, 42, NEW BOND ST. W.

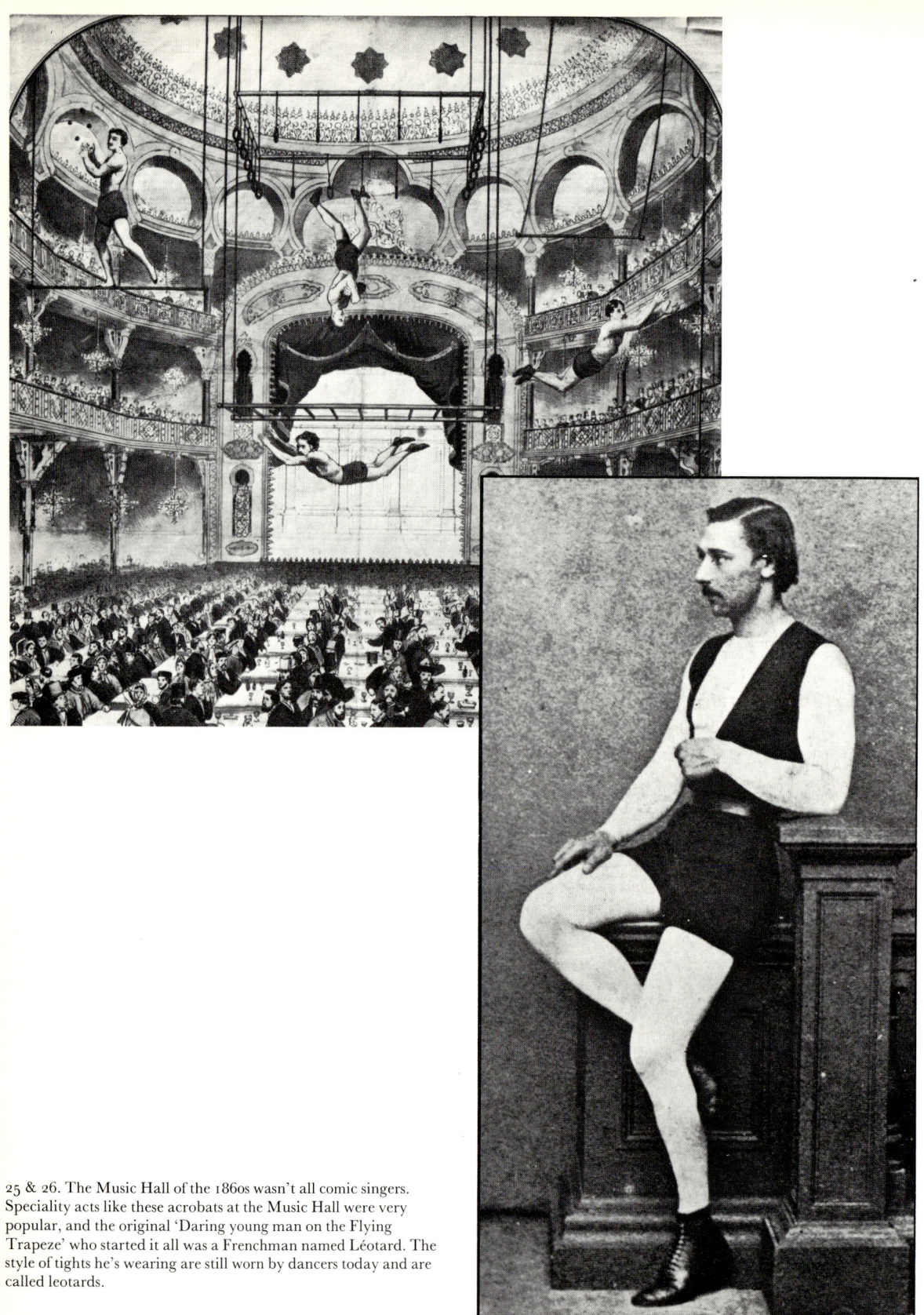

25 & 26. The Music Hall of the 1860s wasn't all comic singers. Speciality acts like these acrobats at the Music Hall were very popular, and the original 'Daring young man on the Flying Trapeze' who started it all was a Frenchman named Léotard. The style of tights he's wearing are still worn by dancers today and are called leotards.

27. Seaside songs were popular as early as the 1860s. 'On the Sands' was written (to the tune of 'Dixie') for Billy Randall by John Caulfield, who was the chairman at the Canterbury Hall.

28. Seaside entertainers, Southsea, 1890s. Many stars have started this way.

29 & 30. Arthur Lloyd (1840–1904). The forerunner of the 'lions comiques' (more about them later). He was one of the first music-hall stars to appear, privately, before Royalty. 'Married to a Mermaid' (*left*) and 'Not for Joseph' (*above*) were two of Lloyd's 'hits'.

The phrase 'Lion Comique' was first used in reference to George Leybourne (1842–1884) by J. J. Poole, the then manager of the Metropolitan Music Hall, Edgware Road. What exactly it meant I have no idea, but it has such a rare ring of individual richness that it describes what Leybourne was all about perfectly.

The arrival of Leybourne on the London scene, from the Midlands in 1865, started the whole 'Good Old Days' view of Music Hall.

Most comic singers, up till then, had presented 'character' songs; Leybourne relied (with rare exceptions, e.g. 'The Mousetrap man') on just one character, his own. The enterprising 'guvnor' of the Canterbury, at that time William Holland, noted Leybourne's good looks, fine magnetic voice and natural stage presence and encouraged him to present the 'heavy swell' image on and off stage. His biggest song, 'Champagne Charlie', gives you the whole picture. He personified the ideal, the jolly, hard-drinking, never-go-to-bed, pots-of-money, man-about-town. He travelled to and from the halls in a carriage drawn by four white horses (supplied by Holland) and when in public ordered only champagne (paid for by Moet & Chandon).

The cult of the personality had begun.

L/=

Gilbert Hastings Macdermott—'The Great Macdermott' (1845–1901).
A star who is included in every book on Music Hall for just one reason, his singing of 'We Don't Want to Fight But By Jingo if We Do'. A song which made up people's minds for them on a particularly ticklish foreign affair. In 1877 opinions were split as to whether England should support Russia or Turkey. The arguments went on and on until one night at the old London Pavilion (*right*) G.H. advanced to the footlights, struck a warlike posture, and, in his powerful and melodramatic manner, began . . .

> The dogs of war are loose
> And the ragged Russian Bear
> Full bent on blood and robbery
> Has crawled out of his lair . . .

This was just the stuff the audience wanted to hear and the chorus was even better—

> We don't want to fight but by Jingo if we do
> We've got the ships, we've got the men, we've got
>   the money too
> We've fought the bear before
> And while we're Britons true—

(and imagine this final line delivered full blast with all the power that only a highly successful melodrama player, which G.H. originally was, could muster).

THE RUSSIANS SHALL NOT HAVE CONSTANTINOPLE!

That was it, no contest. The song was a riot, sung everywhere, at political meetings, in peoples homes; it was even issued (words and music) as a supplement to the Paris Figaro. The whole business was speedily cleared up and a new word was added to the English language—'Jingoism'. The man who wrote the song, G. W. Hunt, was a hero. The Great Macdermott gave him a guinea for it!

MR. G. H. MACDERMOTT.
No Theatres for him at Christmas; he nails his Colours to the Music-Hall Mast.

35 & 36. G. H. Macdermott remained a star for many years at the
London Pavilion and added other phrases to our language with
'Dear Old Pals' and 'Here comes the Bogie Man'.

MACDERMOTTS LAST NEW SONG.

ANOTHER FELLAH'S

WRITTEN BY

COMPOSED BY

GEORGE DANCE, ERNEST J. SYMONS,

SUNG WITH THE GREATEST SUCCESS
BY

G. H. MACDERMOTT.

ENT. STA. HALL.

PR. 4/-

LONDON;
HOPWOOD & CREW 42 NEW BOND ST. W.

DAN LOWREY'S
MUSIC ★ HALL!

DAME STREET,
Entrance to Boxes, New Pit Stalls
and Balcony,
SYCAMORE STREET.

DUBLIN.
[Entrance to Balcony and
Top Gallery,
CRAMPTON COURT.

MONDAY, FEBRUARY 4th, 1884.

Important and expensive engagement for Six Nights only of the Great A. G.

VANCE!
IN HIS IMPERSONATIONS.

First Appearance at this Hall of Miss MARIE

...INARD

Character Vocalist.

...Appearance of RICHARD

...LES!!

...omic Vocalist, Author and Composer.

...rst Appearance of Miss

...LENORE

...g and Pump Dancer.   Champion Lady Slab Dancer of the World !!!

...rn visit of the Celebrated

...TROUPE.

f their visit here.

VANCE'S VARIETIES
EGYPTIAN HALL.

EVERY EVENING AT EIGHT

EVERY
WEDNESDAY and SATURDAY at THREE and EIGHT.

37, 38 & 39. Leybourne's big rival was Alfred 'The Great' Vance
(1840–1889). Vance, though (an ex-actor), was a much more
versatile performer, playing as many as twenty different
characters in his one-man show. Perhaps this lack of definite
personality is why he is not so remembered as the flashier
Leybourne.

40 & 41. Jenny Hill (1850–1896) 'The Vital Spark'. One of the first big female stars. She started as a child performer at the Doctor Johnson Concert Room, Bolt Court, Fleet Street in the 1860s, singing comic songs but excelling in pathetic roles. She had a most beautiful song in 'The Boy I Love is up in the Gallery'.

ROYAL YORK
MUSIC HALL,
ABOVE BAR, SOUTHAMPTON.

Proprietress - Mrs. G. HYLES. | Manager - Mr. H. CHURCH.
Doors open at 7.15, Entertainments to commence at 7.45.
Saturdays and Holidays the Doors will open at 7, to commence at 7.30.
The TRAM CARS pass the doors, the last leaving at Eleven p.m.

ON MONDAY, OCTOBER 4, 1880.
AND EVERY EVENING DURING THE WEEK.

Enormous Success and Last Six Nights of Miss

JENNY HILL!
THE VITAL SPARK.

Cheered Nightly, Deservedly Cheered; Her Character Impersonations abound
with pleasing Merriment and lively Effusions of Wit and Humour.

Monday Night first time of the Great Satirical and Topical Character Imper-
sonation of MEPHISTOPHELES. Miss HILL will also during this, the
Last Week of her Engagement, introduce numerous popular Songs and
Character Impersonations as made so celebrated by her.

First appearance and for Six Nights only of Mr. GEORGE

GEORGE VOKES
Comic Vocalist and Dancer.

First Appearance this Season of Miss FLORRIE

DESMOND
Serio-Comic, Characteristic and Dancer.

First Appearance in Southampton of the SISTERS

42. The London Pavilion, 1898. The new hall which succeeded the roofed-over stable yard shown on page 41. The exterior's exactly the same today.

Moonlight.
Distant Voices.

43, 44 & 45. An Interesting Trio. *Above*: Artistes in the wings at
the Royal Holborn, 1902. The 'turns' were working four or five
halls a night all over town, hence one communal changing place.
Opposite above: How about that for good business! *Right*: A fair
summing-up of the standard types of 'turn'.

BEFORE THE DOORS OPEN
(LONDON PAVILION).

THE LANGUAGE OF THE MUSIC-HALL.

Navigation. Travel.
eparting or Returning
over (Soldier or Sailor).

Affair of the Heart.
Patriotic Fervour.

Lodgers. Mothers-in-law.
Drink. Kippers.

Any reference to Paris,
Ostend, the Continent.

A Quintet of lovely ladies of the halls. *This page top*: Cissie Loftus (1876–1943): Impressionist on the halls and a highly successful straight actress. *Bottom*: Bessie Bellwood (1857–1896): a singer of cockney songs and a wild woman. *Opposite page top*: Lottie Collins (1866–1910): The singer and dancer of 'Ta-ra-ra-boom-de-ay!' *Middle*: Lily Burnard. 'Two Little Girls in Blue' was her big hit. *Bottom*: Vesta Victoria (1874–1951): Singer of so many famous songs—'Waiting at the Church', 'Our Lodger's Such a nice Young Man', and 'Daddy wouldn't buy me a Bow Wow'.

Marie Lloyd (1870–1922) 'The Queen Of The Music Hall'.

Mention Music Hall to almost anyone and Marie Lloyd is the name they'll remember. Hers are the songs that have become 'folk' music. 'My Old Man said Follow the Van' ('The Cock Linnet Song'), 'Oh Mr Porter', 'One of the Ruins that Cromwell Knocked about a bit', and 'A Little of what you fancy does you good'. Go to a 'knees up' in London, or anywhere else in England for that matter, and sooner or later you'll hear Marie's songs. They are good songs sure, but they're something else. They bring back another age, an age when moonlight flits and getting boozed were everyday occurrences, an age when problems were basic and human.

Marie Lloyd herself was basic and human.

She was a cockney, a star at sixteen, Drury Lane's principal girl at twenty-one and was a smash hit everywhere, yet she stayed a cockney.

She saw things only in black and white, she was an 'easy touch', great at her job, expansive, explosive and loved by everyone who knew her. ''nuff said'?

In 1936 Naomi Jacob wrote a brilliant biography called *Our Marie*: please read it; it's the best book on a music-hall personality ever written.

Yours always
Marie Lloyd

53. Here's Marie (second from left) in a rare genteel mood with three of her seven sisters (Alice, Grace and Annie).

54. My favourite picture of 'Our Marie': a posed 'pin up'.

55. Another favourite: relaxing at home in 1914.

56. Charles Coborn (1852–1945). A star with two immortal songs – 'Two Lovley Black Eyes' and 'The Man Who Broke The Bank at Monte Carlo'. He's seen here with his daughter in 1911 'putting himself about' to improve the lot of music hall performers – something he did all his life. His autobiography *The Man Who Broke the Bank at Monte Carlo* is well worth reading.

37 & 58. *Above left*: Tom Costello (1863–1943). When people think of music-hall stars they often tend to associate them with just one song. Tom Costello's 'Comrades' is a good example, but, like so many of the great stars, he was extremely versatile and is billed on the poster (*left*) as 'Actor, Vocalist, Comedian and Dancer'.
59. The Parthenon Music Hall, Liverpool (*above*) where Tom Costello was working the week of July 19th 1897. This was the tiny theatre where Sir Oswald Stoll started his career as a music-hall manager at 14.

60. The Oxford Music Hall (*Opposite*). Charles Morton's next
triumph after the Canterbury. Topping the bill is Alec Hurley,
Marie Lloyd's second husband.

61 & 62. The Music Hall business soon swept the country and
here are just a couple of the hundreds of provincial theatres.
(*Above*) The Palace Theatre, Lincoln, converted 1902, still stands;
(*Right*) The Empire, Sunderland, built 1907, and still going
strong. Incidentally the Empire houses an excellent Museum of
Music Hall.

Empire Palace of Varieties, Limited.

MIDDLESBROUGH, YORKS.

63. *Above*: Another giant provincial hall. Sadly, music-hall history outside London is poorly documented. I have found one good book on the subject though: *Northern Music Hall* by G. Mellor.

WHISTLING THE LAST
NEW TUNE.

Vesta Tilley (1864–1952) 'The London Idol'.
Vesta Tilley and Marie Lloyd were the two biggest
female stars of the era, yet couldn't have been more
different, onstage or off. Marie was essentially
female while Vesta Tilley's whole career was based
on dressing up as a man.

She first went into 'drag' at the age of three-and-a-
half during a benefit performance for her father (the
Chairman of a small Music Hall in Gloucester).
With rare exceptions she maintained her male
characterisations till her farewell performance at
the London Coliseum in 1920. Her portrayals, which
were perfect in every detail of dress and mannerism,
ranged from the tipsy 'swell' of 'Following in Father's
Footsteps' to the upright patriot of 'Jolly Good Luck
To The Girl who Loves a Soldier'.

Poor Marie Lloyd's private life was, to say the
least, stormy, whereas Vesta Tilley's was a bed of
roses. She was adored and courted by the 'best'
young men-about-town, eventually marrying Walter
de Frece (a music-hall manager who became an M.P.
On second thoughts perhaps not such a big step!).
Rumour says Sir Oswald Stoll, a close friend of
Vesta's, introduced de Frece to her, which prompted
Gus Elen to sing 'Never introduce your Donah (girl
friend) To a Pal!!' Walter de Frece was eventually
knighted, and, as Lady de Frece, the London Idol
spent a blissful retirement twixt Maidenhead and
Monte Carlo.

65. A rare photograph of the beautiful Lady de Frece as herself.

175 E   VESTA TILLEY.   ROTARY PHOTO E.C.

PHILCO SERIES 3116 D   VESTA TILLEY

66, 67, 68 & 69. A quartet of Vesta Tilley's 'Blokes'. Today the whole idea of male impersonation may seem slightly 'kinky' but it, and Vesta Tilley, were fantastically popular. At the height of her powers she was a setter of male fashion. Men would ask their tailors for outfits just like hers.

VESTA TILLEY   PHOTO HANA

VESTA TILLEY.   175 C.

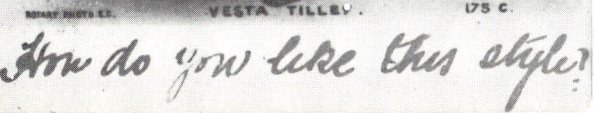

How do you like this style?

70. George Dance, who wrote this song for Vesta Tilley, later
became Sir George Dance, but not before he'd also written 'Come
Where the Booze is Cheaper'.

71. The Empire Theatre, Leicester Square, in 1902, the year of
Edward VII's coronation.

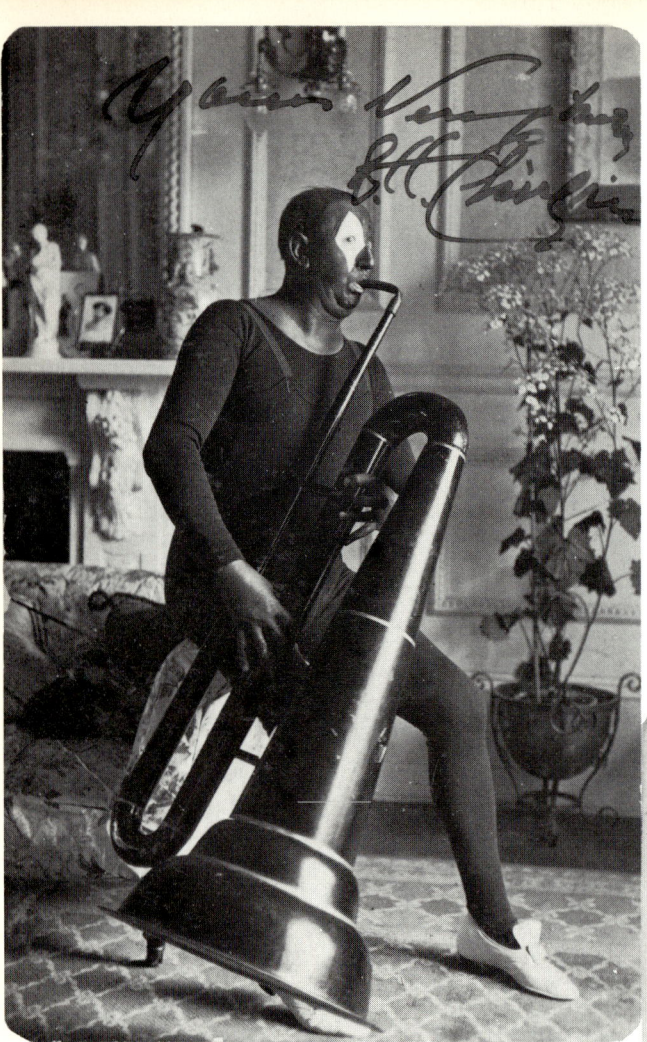

72. (*left*) G. H. Chirgwin (1855–1922) 'The White Eyed Kaffir'.
A very popular multi-instrumentalist and entertainer.
   How audiences could take his two hit songs (both dramatic ballads) 'The Blind Boy' and 'My Fiddle Is my Sweetheart' seriously when he looked like this I'll never know. But they're good songs.
73. (*Below*) Paul Cinquevalli (1859–1918).
For 20 years the undisputed King of music-hall jugglers.

The "VARIETY" Stage.   PAUL CINQUEVALLI.

74 & 75. The visits of music hall stars to America began before the days of Sam Cowell (see *The Cowells in America* by M. Willson Disher). (*Left*) An interesting photograph of George Lashwood's visit in 1911. His most famous song was the beautiful 'In the Twi Twi Twilight'.

PHILCO SERIES 3383 C   MR GEORGE LASHWOOD.

76. George Formby (1880–1921). The famous father of ukelele man George Formby junior.

77. Formby Senior cutting a record encouraged by the famous opera singer Tetrazzini. On being faced with this equipment Dan Leno commented, 'How the hell can I be funny into a funnel?! – How could anyone?

78. Arthur Roberts (1853–1933). An early music-hall comic who left the halls to become a musical comedy legend.

79. The shape of things to come. (*Below*) Moving Pictures were top of the Bill in 1898. (*Right*) Revue was thoroughly established by 1913.

☀ PROGRAMME. ☀

1.   **Miss M. DANVERS,**
The Charming Tyrolean Vocalist.

2.   **Miss L. ARMSTRONG,**
The Vocal Wonder.

3.   **Mr. T. STUART,**
The Popular Mimic.

4.   **Mr. CYRUS DARE,**
The Royal Society Entertainer with Musical Sketches.

5.   **Mr. LESLIE KING,**
The Celebrated English Baritone
(Direct from the Empire Theatre, Leicester Square).

6.   **Mr. W. MOORE,**
Entertainer and Reciter.

7.   **Professor ROUSBY'S**
Illustrated Ballads with Limelight Effects.

8.   A Great Musical Treat—
PAGANINI REDIVIVUS,
The most highly-talented Musical Genius in the World.
This wonderful Violinist has had the distinguished honour on several occasions of appearing before Her Most Gracious Majesty Queen Victoria, H.R.H. the Prince of Wales, H.R.H. the Duke of Edinburgh.

9.   **CAPTAIN SHAW'S**
Life-sized Animated Photography,
Showing all the Latest and Most Popular Pictures, including the
SPANISH-AMERICAN WAR:
Also the Magnificent and Most Realistic Pageant of
Gladstone's Funeral.

These Entertainments are under the sole management of Mr. Victor Roi.

ST. GEORGE'S HALL,
CANTERBURY.

Special Attraction for Cricket Week,
Commencing August 1st and during the Week.

Special Engagement by Mr. Victor Roi of

Mr. R. A. ROBERTS,
FROM

MASKELYNE AND COOKE'S,
The Premier Entertainer,
Facial Impersonator,
and Quick Change Artist,
IN HIS

Original and Refined Selections,
As performed by him for THREE YEARS,

1,800 CONSECUTIVE TIMES AT
THE EGYPTIAN HALL, LONDON,
Supported by his

Comedy ⹀ Entertainment Company,

Mr. OLDBURY BROUGH, Musical Director and Solo Pianist.
Miss NANCE HOROBIN, Mezzo Soprano.
Mr. PAUL K. PRANTZA,
The Eminent Illusionist, Conjuror, and Ventriloquist.
Mr. CYRIL OAKES, Comedian.
Mr. KENNERLY CRANSTON in his Musical Grotesque Scena.

HULLO, RAG-TIME!

HIPPODROME REVUE

Albert Chevalier (1861–1923).

It's strange that one of the immortal music-hall cockneys wasn't a cockney at all. He was born in the, then, fairly posh Notting Hill area of London to a family who wanted him to become a priest.

He reluctantly went on the halls after fourteen years as a straight actor (today it's usually the other way round). Friends persuaded him the cockney characterisations he did for them in private would go well with a wider audience. They did, and his two songs 'Knocked 'Em In The Old Kent Road' and 'My Old Dutch' became classics and are still very much sung today.

Though he was christened 'The Costers' Laureate', and topped bills all over London, he never really enjoyed Music Hall. In fact he was 'a turn' for only a few years; most of his career was spent touring his highly successful one-man show. The host of different characters he played in these recitals were much more to his liking.

In his autobiography, *Before I Forget*, his comments on the difference between legitimate theatre and Music Hall still hold good today:

'What makes it so difficult and interesting to produce effects artistically and legitimately in a Music Hall is that you are never quite certain of your audience. One tipsy man in the gallery is sufficient to upset all your calculations.'

So say all of us!

81. (*Right*) Mr Albert Chevalier, actor.

QUEEN'S HALL
LANGHAM PLACE, W.

Mr. ALBERT

CHEVALIER

GIVES

RECITALS

EVERY AFTERNOON AT THREE

AND ALSO

THURSDAYS & SATURDAYS at 8.30

(Under the management of Mr. Robert Newman).

▶▶▶▶▶▶▶▶▶

Tickets, Numbered & Reserved, 7/6 & 5/-; Unnumbered, 2/6 & 1/-

Of Ashton, 38 Old Bond Street; Chappell & Co., 50 New Bond Street; Gastrell, 13 Sussex Place, South Kensington; Hays, 26 Old Bond Street and 4 Royal Exchange Buildings, E.C.; Keith, Prowse, & Co., 48 Cheapside, 167 New Bond Street (late Bobb's), and all Branches; Lacon & Ollier, 166a New Bond Street; Mitchell's Royal Libraries, 33 Old Bond Street, 16 Gloucester Road, S.W., and 3 Leadenhall Street, E.C.; Stanley Lucas, Weber, & Co., 84 New Bond Street; St. James's Hall Ticket Office; the usual agents; Army and Navy Stores; Civil Service Stores; Whiteley's Stores; Harrod's Stores; District Messenger Offices; and at
Robert Newman's Box Office, Queen's Hall, Langham Place, W.

83. Chevalier in 'The Future Mrs Awkins'.

'Little Tich' (1868–1928).

Another word the Music Hall gave the English
Language, 'Tich' for someone small. The original
Little Tich (Harry Relph) was very small and took
his name from the Tichborne Claimant in a famous
court case of the period. The Tichborne Claimant
was a huge fat man so Harry Relph called himself
Little Tichborne, this being eventually shortened to
Little Tich.

Little Tich (like all highly individual comics) is
extremely difficult to assess as again 'it wasn't what
he said it was the way he said it,' or rather, in his case
'the way he *did* it'.

He left no memorable songs behind and one has to
rely on contemporary reports. These all mention his
multitude of characters and his incredible com-
mand of half-a-dozen different languages. He was as
popular on the continent as in Britain. However, it
was his visual appeal that made the greatest impact
and there is still in existence a fabulous piece of film
showing him, in his big boots (see the poster opposite), performing his incredible dance. I've shown
this film to teenagers and it had them rolling on the
floor. It is very very funny.

84. A poster typical of the sort performers hung outside the
theatres they were working. The phrase 'One Tich of Nature
makes the whole world Grin' was invented by H. Chance Newton,
author of a mighty tome, *Idols of the 'Halls'*.

85. The Tivoli Music Hall London (1910). Notice the reference to Dr Crippen on the newsboys' placards and the sign 'Living Pictures' on right of picture. 'Living Pictures' were the forerunners of the nude tableaux which helped kill variety in the late 1950s.
86. (*Inset*) The Tichborne Claimant himself appeared in the Music Halls and did no better there than he did in the courtrooms.

After which, (about 9.15 o'clock,)

THE TICHBORNE CLAIMANT

Will address the Audience upon the TICHBORNE CASE, upon the TRIALS, upon JURIES, and upon various incidents of HIS PRISON LIFE.

The Performances will conclude with the pathetic Military Drama, by J. T. HAINES, Esq., entitled THE

SOLDIER'S BRIDE

Or, The Battle of Austerlitz!
(*A French Story of 1805.*)

Colonel Le Froi	Mr. J. C. Howard
Jean Phillipe Rose	Mr. E. Drayton
Index	Mr. G. B. Bigwood
Charles Merlet	Mr. E. Newbound
Everard St. Louis	Mr. W. Steadman
Peter Pontoon	Mr. G. Lewis
Phillipe Marcel	Mr. J. B. Howe
Ernest	Miss Ada Morgan
Graspeau	Mr. J. Reynolds
Deaf Martin	Mr. Barrett
Constance De Merville	Miss Elise Grey
Merial Bombelle	Miss Lizzie Howe
Dame Canteen	Miss M. Pettifer

Soldiers—French and German, Female Peasants, &c., &c.

Act 1.—The Conscription !

Act 2.—The Soldier's Bride !!

Act 3.—The Billet of the Bullet!!·

Three great music-hall stars I had the pleasure of seeing.
87. (*Above*) Randolph Sutton (1889–1969) (his Mother Kelly's
Doorstep' is still popular), and Nellie Wallace (1870–1948) (a
genuinely funny lady).
88. (*Right*) Gertie Gitana (1889–1957). 'Nelly Dean' was her big
song and it always saddened her to hear it being mangled through
the doors of public houses.
89 & 90 (*Opposite*) Sir George Robey (1869–1954). 'The Prime
Minister of Mirth'. One of the great music-hall figures. A highly
individual 'stand up' comedian and comedy actor. Try and read
more about his marvellous career in *Looking Back on Life* by
George Robey, 1933.

McGLENNON'S AUTHORISED EDITION.   PRICE ONE PENNY.

THE ECCENTRIC
GEORGE ROBEY'S
SONG BOOK.

CONTENTS:

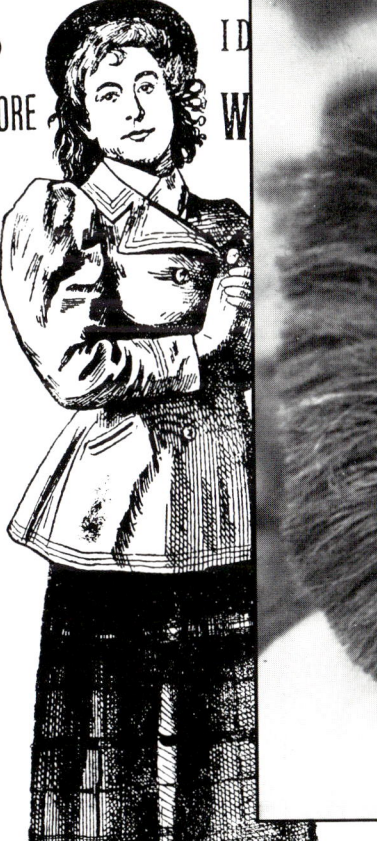

MR. GEORGE ROBEY.

HAPPY FANNY FIELDS.   3503

91. (*Left*) 'Happy' Fanny Fields (1881–1961). A popular American import to the British Halls.
92. (*Below*) Harry Fragson (1866–1913). A popular piano entertainer. He worked with a French accent in London and a cockney accent in Paris.
93. (*Opposite Bottom*) Jack Pleasants (1875–1924). Specialised in playing the 'daft' Northerner. He first sang 'I'm Twenty One Today' and 'I'm Shy Mary Ellen I'm Shy'.
94. (*Opposite Top*) Sir Harry Lauder (1870–1950). One of the few Scots to make it big on the Halls. He became an international star, had dozens of hit songs and with George Robey was only the second music-hall performer to be knighted.

1286 A   MR. HARRY FRAGSON.   ROTARY PHOTO. E.C.

To Lloyd and Montrose, with kindest regards from Jack Pleasants

0/5196

ROTARY PHOTO

Wee Georgie Wood

95 (*Left*) R. G. Knowles (1861–1919). An American 'patter'
comic who had a big success in England. A great ad libber, he
remarked once when a cat walked across the stage during his act –
'This is supposed to be a monologue not a catalogue'. He told his
life story in *A Modern Columbus*.
96. (*Above*) 'Wee' Georgie Wood. A sketch comedian 'par
excellence' and a brother Water Rat. He topped bills for many
years with his small-boy sketches and now tops bills as himself.

MAUDE MORTIMER, THE ORIGINAL LADY SINGER OF "TIPPERARY,"
will devote every penny realised by the sale of these postcards
to the purchase of cigarettes for our gallant 'boys' at the Front.

This Page Two 'Original' singers of 'It's a long way to Tipperary'.
97. (*Top*) Maude Mortimer, I can find nothing about (it's things like this that drive you crazy when you get involved in music-hall history).
98. (*Bottom*) Florrie Forde (1876–1940) of course was the great Australian chorus singer who had so many hits including 'Kelly From The Isle of Man', 'Pack Up Your Troubles In Your Old Kit Bag', 'Down At The Old Bull & Bush', and, I'm inclined to take her word for it, 'Tipperary'.
99. (*Opposite*) John Tiller's 'Superba' Quartet. Some of the forerunners of the famous Tiller Girls. Today their routines have hardly changed from the original guardsmanlike conception.

FLORRIE FORDE
THE ORIGINAL SINGER OF "TIPPERARY."

100. (*Above*) Harry Champion (1866–1942). Another artiste whose songs added to our language – 'Any Old Iron', 'Ginger You're Barmy', 'Boiled Beef and Carrots' and many more all sung at breakneck speed.

101. (*Opposite Top*) Harry Tate (1873–1940). Famous for his sketches e.g. 'Motoring', which was recorded and is still very funny.

102. (*Opposite Bottom*) Billy Merson (1881–1947). With his most famous song. When Al Jolson performed the number Billy Merson tried to get payment for it but lost the case. *Fixing the Stoof Oop*, his autobiography, tells of his fascinating career through circus, variety and musical comedy.

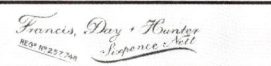

Francis, Day & Hunter
No. 746. SIXPENNY POPULAR EDITION. (NO DISCOUNT ALLOWED)
This Song may be Sung in Public without Fee or License, except at Theatres and Music Halls, which Rights are reserved. For Pantomime permissions apply to Francis, Day & Hunter.

THE SPANIARD THAT BLIGHTED MY LIFE.

WRITTEN, COMPOSED AND SUNG BY

BILLY MERSON.

London:
FRANCIS, DAY & HUNTER.
142, Charing Cross Road & 22, Denmark Street, W.C.
New York: T.B. HARMS & FRANCIS, DAY & HUNTER, INC., 62-64, West 45th Street.

Copyright MCMXI, in the United States of America by Francis, Day & Hunter.

103. Dan Leno (*Bottom*) with Johnny Danvers (*Middle*) and
Herbert Campbell (*Top*) during his sixteen-year pantomime reign
at Drury Lane Theatre.

Dan Leno (1861–1904).
To me the most fascinating character in the whole of music-hall history. He left no memorable songs but he did leave (in *Dan Leno—Hys Booke*) some wild, unforgettable, fantasy-packed patter. It's a cross between Spike Milligan, Stephen Leacock and Edward Lear and as funny to read as to perform.

He was 'born in a trunk' and on the boards while still an infant. In 1869 Charles Dickens saw him perform and told him 'Good little man you'll make headway'. He did and was in turn a contortionist, champion clog dancer, comic singer, the greatest pantomime dame and finally the one and only Dan Leno.

He became the most popular comedian of the age. In fact his popularity and constant inventiveness caused his early death in a mental home. (On being admitted he looked at a clock and asked 'Is that clock right?' On being told it was he replied 'Well what's it doing in here then?')

The only way we can judge this strange and brilliant man now is, once again, by contemporary reviews. This is from the normally cold and clinical Max Beerbohm: 'I defy anyone not to have loved Dan Leno at first sight. The moment he skipped onto the stage all hearts were his, we were aware that here was a man unlike anyone else we had seen, here was a creature apart radiating an ethereal essence all his own.'

A very good collection of quotes on all aspects of Music Hall is *Music Hall in Britain* by David Cheshire, and a fabulous collection of photographs are in *British Music Hall* by Raymond Mander and Joe Mitchenson.

To my old chum
Herbert with kindest
wishes for old times
sake from Dan Leno.

104. Max Beerbohm on Dan Leno again: 'That face so tragic
with all the tragedy that is writ on the face of a baby monkey
yet ever liable to relax its mouth into a sudden wide grin and
to screw up its eyes to vanishing point over some little triumph
wrested from fate.'

THE MIDNIGHT MARCH

WRITTEN AND COMPOSED BY
FRED. GILBERT,

Sung with Unbounded Success

BY

DAN LENO

IN SIR AUGUSTUS HARRIS'S PANTOMIME
"LITTLE BO-PEEP, LITTLE RED RIDING HOOD, & HOP O' MY THUMB"
AT

106, 107, 108 & 109. A quartet of famous Leno characters. The
one above, Richard the Third, he never played but longed to.
After he'd explained to Sir Herbert Beerbohm Tree just how he
would play the part, Tree commented: 'If Dan Leno plays
Richard the Third it will be the greatest performance of the part
we have ever seen'.

110. (*Right below*) The belt he won in a competition to find 'The
Champion Clog Dancer of the World'.

MUSIC HALL PROPRIETOR.

112. The London Coliseum (designed by Frank Matcham 1852–1920). Opened in 1904. Now a home of ballet and opera, it is forever linked with its builder, Sir Oswald Stoll.

Sir Oswald Stoll (1866–1942)

With Charles Morton (the builder of the Canterbury Music Hall) the most famous music-hall proprietor of them all.

He was brought up in the business, being taken away from school to run his late father's establishment, The Parthenon Music Hall, Liverpool. At fourteen he was the manager, booker, scene painter and everything else. He prospered and within a few short years owned eight variety theatres and became chairman and managing director of the great Moss Empire Theatre chain.

His dream of a Music Hall in London came true with his building of the Coliseum. The way he chose the site for the theatre seems to be typical of his painstaking, methodical approach to business. Armed with notebook and pencil he studied various spots in London to find just where the greatest number of visitors passed. Charing Cross was the place and he bought the nearest available site at the bottom of St Martin's Lane.

The opening of his new theatre, with its four shows a day, really meant the end of the old-style halls. The Coliseum was respectable and Stoll's policy was 'refined' entertainment. The late Sophie Tucker, after a row with him, said, 'Mr Stoll, you shouldn't be the manager of a vaudeville theatre. You should be a bishop'. Perhaps, but what a cathedral he left us. He vetted every act himself and anything he considered 'infradig' he stamped on.

For more about Stoll and his theatre read *The House That Stoll Built* by Felix Barker.

114. The First Royal Performance. As Oswald Stoll said in an uncharacteristic outburst, 'The Cinderella of the arts has gone to the ball at last'. Alas, by the time she got there the dance was nearly over. Revue was beginning to take a hold and variety was 'in'.

However, a flip through the next few pages shows us a bill I'd give a T.V. series to have seen.

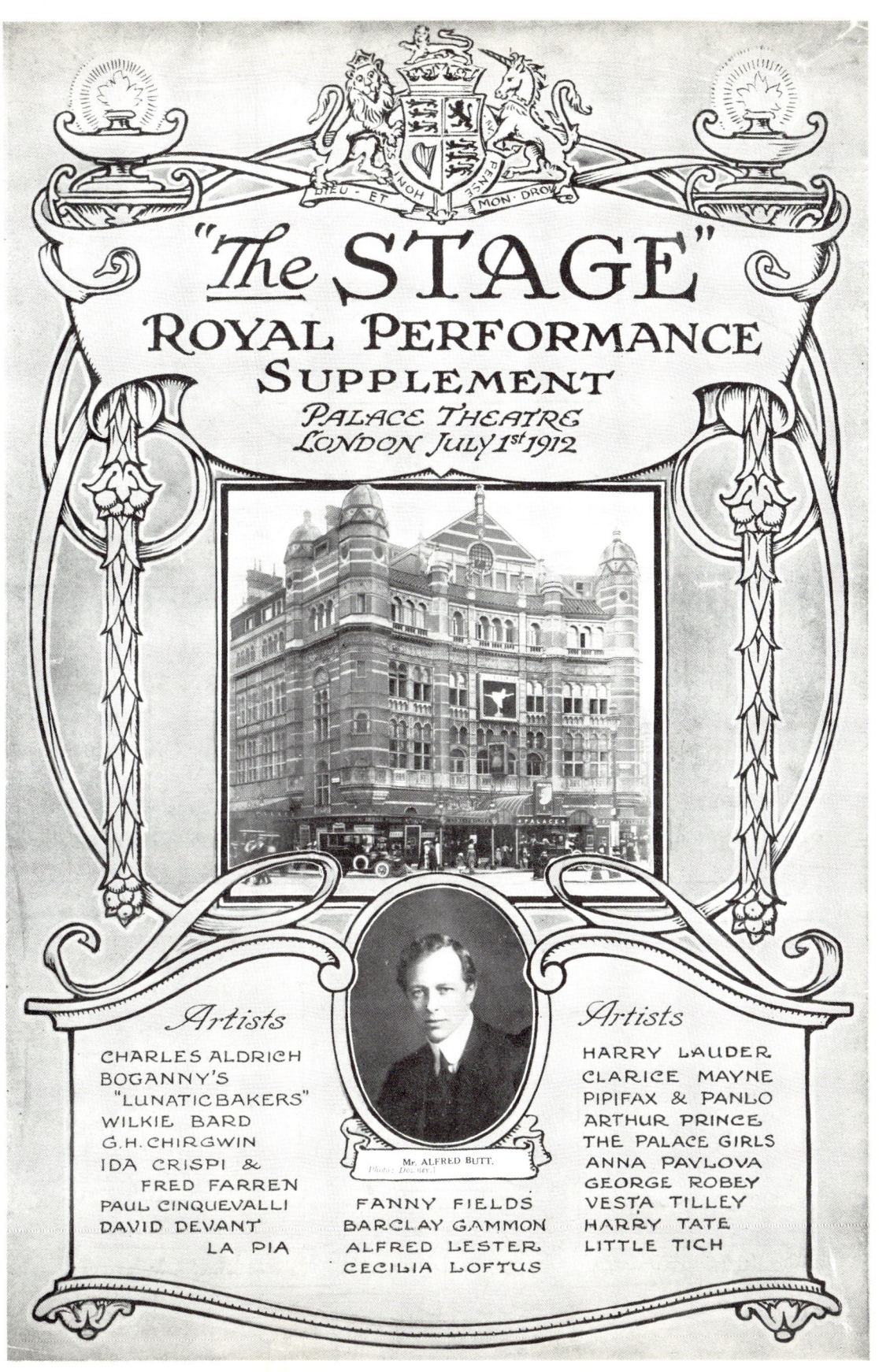

"The STAGE"
ROYAL PERFORMANCE
SUPPLEMENT
PALACE THEATRE
LONDON JULY 1st 1912

Mr. ALFRED BUTT.
Photo: Dover.

Artists

CHARLES ALDRICH
BOGANNY'S
"LUNATIC BAKERS"
WILKIE BARD
G. H. CHIRGWIN
IDA CRISPI &
   FRED FARREN
PAUL CINQUEVALLI
DAVID DEVANT
   LA PIA

FANNY FIELDS
BARCLAY GAMMON
ALFRED LESTER
CECILIA LOFTUS

Artists

HARRY LAUDER
CLARICE MAYNE
PIPIFAX & PANLO
ARTHUR PRINCE
THE PALACE GIRLS
ANNA PAVLOVA
GEORGE ROBEY
VESTA TILLEY
HARRY TATE
LITTLE TICH

CRISPI and FARREN in "The Yankee Tangle."

CLARICE MAYNE

LA PIA
as "The Spirit of the Waves."

Mme. ANNA PAVLOVA.

Mr. BARD in character.

Mr. CHARLES ALDRICH
as a Tramp Juggler.

JOE BOGANNY'S Opium Fiends.

THE PALACE GIRLS.
Misses Cairns, Dolan, Loraine, McSpirit, Oliver, Shaw, Wharton (Captain), Whiting.

Mr. ARTHUR PRINCE.

Mr. BARCLAY GAMMON.

PIPIFAX.

PANLO.

Mr. ALFRED LESTER
as "The Village Fireman,"

Mr. DEVANT in a favourite part, the old
bachelor in "St. Valentine's Eve."

THE NEW ACT DROP.   ["Daily Sketch" Photo.

Photo:] Mr. HERRMANN FINCK,   [Bassano.
Musical Director

In the above picture of "Variety's Garden Party" (which was necessarily taken at the Dress Rehearsal) the following artists are included :—

[Hana.

Martin Adeson, Albert and Edmunds, Charles T. Aldrich, Alexandra and Hughes, Athas and Collins, Charles Austin, Wilkie Bard, Edwin Barwick, George Bastow, Beattie and Babs, Clara Bernard, Billie Bint, Harry Blake, Joe Boganny, Marguerite Broadfoote, Papa Brown, Arthur Carlton, Kate Carney, Dave Carter, Ada Cerito, Harry Champion, G. H. Chirgwin, W. J. Churchill, Paul Cinquevalli, Harry Claff and Alice Tremayne, Tom Clare, Charles Coborn, Ida Crispi and Fred Farren, Flora Cromer, Alf. Cruickshank, Fred Curran, Alexandra Dagmar, Herbert Darnley, George D'Albert, Emilie D'Alton, Percy and Harry Delevine, David Devant, R. H. Douglass, Downes and Langford, Duncan and Godfrey, T. E. Dunville, Marriott Edgar, Seth and Albert Egbert, Tom Edwards, Gus Elen, Fred Emney, Edith Evelyn, Fanny Fields, James and Elsie Finney, Ed. E. Ford, Florrie Forde, W. F. Frame, Harry Freeman. George French, Arthur Gallimore, Florrie Gallimore, Barclay Gammon, Harry Grattan, George Gray, Fred Herbert, Diana Hope, Sydney James, James and Will Kellino, Marie Kendall, Fred Kitchen, La Pia, Lupino Lane, Harry Lauder, Mary Law, Albert Le Fre, John Le Hay, Arthur Lennard, Bob and Jennie Lennard, Alfred Lester, George Leyton, Cecilia Loftus, Marie Loftus, Jack Lorimer, Lotto, Lilo and Otto, Sisters Micarte, Jack Marks, Charles and Joe McConnell, Fred and Gus McNaughton, Clarice Mayne and J. W. Tate, Walter Munroe, My Fancy, Newham and Latimar, M. Novikoff, Anna Pavlova, Pipifax and Panlo, Arthur Prince, Peggy Pryde. Harry Randall, Ella Retford, Arthur Rigby, George Robey, Irene Rose, J. W. Rowley, Cliff Ryland, F. V. St. Clair, Ella Shields, Sinclair and Whiteford, Ryder Slone, Florence Smithers, Esta Stella, Stelling and Revell, James Stewart, Tom Stuart, Harry Tate, Joe Tennyson, Little Tich, Vesta Tilley, Dean Tribune, Vasco, Harriet Vernon, Harry Weldon, Horace Wheatley, Charles Whittle, Billy Williams, J. W. Wilson and Nellie Waring, Tom Woottwell.

KETTNER'S RESTAURANT.
Table d'Hôte Luncheons, Dinners and Suppers, and à la Carte.
(Opposite stage entrance of this Theatre.)

THE
PALACE THEATRE OF VARIETIES

Manager	-	-	Mr. CHARLES MORTON.
Assistant Manager and Treasurer			Mr. PHILIP YORKE.

12/12/98.

Programme   6d.

1.	OVERTURE	"Der Freischutz"	Weber.	7.45
2.	LA TOSTIA. Mandolinist.			7.52
3.	TOM CRAVEN. Comedian.			8.1
4.	CYRUS DARE. Vocal Comedian.			8.13
5.	HARRY PLEON. Comedian.			8.21
6.	ARTHUR NELSTONE AND MINNIE ABBEY.			8.38
	Sketch Artistes.			
7.	EUTERPEAN VOCAL QUARTETTE.			8.44
	Miss ANNIE SWINFEN, Miss ANNIE WILSON,			
	Mr. AGER GROVER, Mr. MUSGROVE TUFNAIL.			
8.	W. P. DEMPSEY. Comedian.			8.52
9.	HARRISON BROCKBANK. Baritone, will sing:			9.2
	(a) "The Bonny Banks of Loch Lomon." ... Scotch Air.			
	(b) "Love, could I only tell Thee" ... Capel.			
10.	SAM LOCKHART'S ELEPHANTS. (The Three Graces.)			9.11
11.	CHARLES CAPPER. Whistler, will perform:			9.35
	(a) "Should he Upbraid?" ... Bishop. (b) "Les Folies Folka" ... Waldteufel.			
12.	MARIE LLOYD. Comedienne.			9.35
13.	BURKE, ANDRUS AND FRISCO (The Broncho Mule). Comedians.			9.49
14.	Orchestral Intermezzo — Overture to "Tannhauser". Wagner.			9.57
15.	WOOD AND SHEPARD. Musical Comedians.			10.9
16.	THE AMERICAN BIOGRAPH.			10.25

Invented by HERMAN CASLER, of New York.

LIST OF PICTURES TO BE SHEWN.

T. F. Dewar's Coach "Basket" passing the
Burford Bridge Hotel, Boxhill.
Companions.
Duel to the Death.
Tug in a Heavy Sea.
Facial Expressions—The Fateful Letter.
Launch of the Worthing Life Boat.
Return.
Launch of H.M. Battleship "Formidable" at
Portsmouth, Nov. 17th, 1898.
Pelicans at the Zoo.
Pussy's Bath.
Antarctic Expedition—Sir George Newnes'
Farewell to Officers and Crew.
From War to Peace—First Departure of s.s.
St. Louis from Southampton, Nov. 5th, 1898.
Fencing Contest from the play "The Three
Musketeers" (by kind permission of Mr.
Lewis Waller).

THE CORONATION OF QUEEN WILHELMINA
OF HOLLAND AT AMSTERDAM—
(a) Arrival of the Queen at the Palace,
Amsterdam, September 5th, 1898.
(b) The Royal Procession to the Church
before the Coronation ceremony.
(c) The Royal Procession from the Church
after the Coronation ceremony.
(d) The Queen and the Queen Mother on the
Palace Balcony responding to the call
of the populace.
Return of Grenadier Guards from the Soudan,
October 8th, 1898. Marching from Waterloo
Station to the Wellington Barracks.
Nelson's Flagship "Victory."
The Strike—His Embarkation at Calais—
Arrival and reception by the Mayor and
Corporation at Dover.
Irish Mail—L.B.W. Railway—Taking up
Water at Pail Speed.
Conway Castle—Panoramic View of Conway
on the L.B.W. Railway.

The Music Composed by ALFRED PLUMPIUS.

17.	CLAN JOHNSTONE DANCERS.	10.55
18.	JOSEPH ARCHER. Comedian.	11.5
19.	THE LEVARDOS. Comedians and Gymnasts.	11.15

MUSICAL DIRECTOR, Mr. ALFRED PLUMPIUS.

The order and composition of this Programme may be varied as circumstances require.

DOORS OPEN 7.40. COMMENCE 7.45.

BOX OFFICE OPEN FROM 11 TO 5. TELEPHONE No 5040 GERRARD.

SATURDAY MATINÉES during December will be given
on DECEMBER 17th and 31st, at Two o'clock.

The Pianofortes used at this Theatre are by Messrs. JOHN BRINSMEAD & SON.
The Mason & Hamlin Organ used at the Theatre is supplied by Messrs. METZLER & CO
POPULAR PRICES—PRIVATE BOXES from 1 to 3½ Guineas. FAUTEUILS numbered and
reserved, 7/6 ORCHESTRA STALLS (numbered and reserved), 5/-
ROYAL CIRCLE, Two First Rows numbered and reserved, 5/- ROYAL CIRCLE (unreserved), 3/-
FIRST CIRCLE, 2/- AMPHITHEATRE 1/-

Application for Advertisements in this Programme to be made to F. KING & CO., Ltd. Advertisement Department, 63, St. Martin's Lane, W.C.

PROGRAMME

SMITH, VAL ROSA & Cº LITH 67, WILSON Sᵗ FINSBURY E.C.

THE GOLDEN DUSTMAN,

OR

Leave us in yer will before yer die.

A SKETCH OF THE FUTURE

Written by

ERIC·GRAHAM,

Composed by

GEORGE·LE·BRUNN,

CHORUS.

But, nah I'm goin' to be a reglar Toff,
   A-ridin' in my carriage and a pair,
A Top-'at on my 'ead, and fevvers in my bed,
   And call meself The Dook o' Barnit Fair.
A sternycan rahnd the bottom 'o my coat,
   A Piccadilly winder in my eye,
Oh! Fancy all the Dustmen a-shoutin' in my yer,
   Leave us in yer Will before yer die.

Sung by

GUS ELEN.

Gus Elen (1862–1940)

Forgive me indulging myself with a couple of pages devoted to the singer of my very favourite music-hall songs.

Gus Elen became the greatest singer of coster songs via an assortment of jobs, programme boy, barman, seller of pigs' trotters and nigger minstrel.

His success was with cockney songs—not the romantic idealised Albert Chevalier type, but the genuine article. He sang songs about real-life situations, songs that went straight to the heart of matters.

When he became a star in the 1890s his coster monger was already a vanishing type; like Sam Weller he even substituted V's for W's. But he and his songs were a smash hit at the Palladium when he made a come back in the 1930s. Why? Because he was the real thing. Imagine the face opposite summing it all up with this little-known song of his.

I ain't at all the Coster wot yer 'ears about in
    songs,
As allus talks about 'is gal, 'er beauty and 'is
    wrongs;
I've neither inclination or the time you may be
    bound,
To go out mashing donahs, and a 'overing around.
And then a serenading when the night is freezing
    'ard
Is a kind of sport I think you'll find the costers
    always barred;
When the elements is wicious on the landlord we
    will sub,
And drink and smoke and sometimes fight inside
    the nearest pub.
But it sounds so wery pretty in a sweetly warbled
    ditty,
With the footlights, limelights, pearlies to the
    ground.
Now I gives you all my word, it's a fable what
    yer've heard,
For there ain't a Coster like it to be found.

119 & 120. Gus Elen's greatest song – the cockney dream of country life. Note the dedication to George R. Sims, whose ballads like 'Christmas Day In The Workhouse' are minor classics too.

Me and 'Er

Written By
Walter Hastings,

Composed By
George Le Brunn.

Sung By
Gus Elen.

London Francis, Day & Hunter, 195, Oxford St. W.
(Publishers of Smallwood's Celebrated Pianoforte Tutor) Smallwood's 55, Melodious Exercises Etc.
New York, T. B. Harms & Co. 18, East 22nd St.
Copyright MDCCCXCIV in the United States of America by Francis, Day & Hunter.

Price 4/-
Copyright

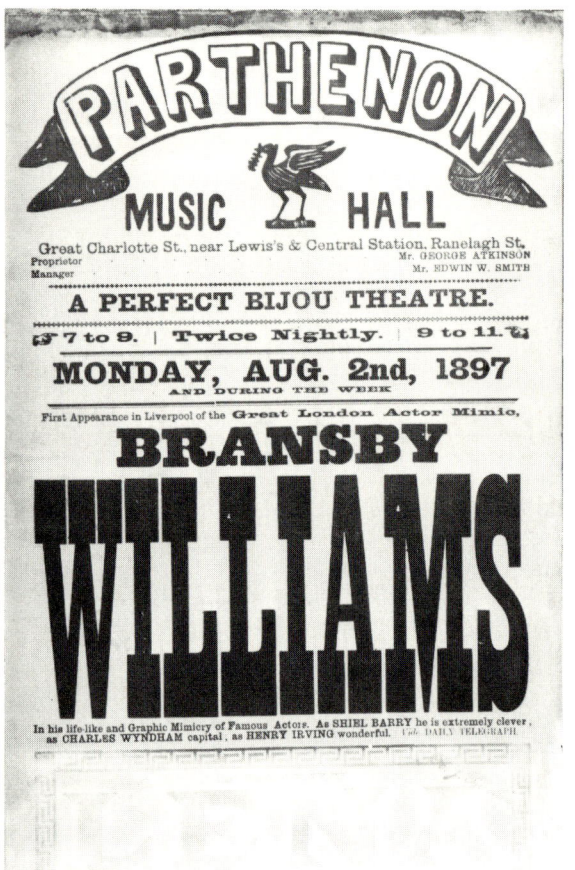

121, 122 & 123. Bransby Williams (1870–1961) and Hetty King (1883–1972). Two stars who did the lot – the halls, variety and television. Bransby Williams (*right*) was topping bills in 1897 and playing Mathias in 'The Bells' on television in 1950. Hetty King (*right inset*) made her first appearance as a male impersonator in 1897 and was top of the bill when she died at 89.

124 & 125. The City Varieties Theatre, Leeds (1865). This beautiful little theatre can be seen regularly on television in the BBC's 'Good Old Days'. Although Music Hall is dead its spirit lives on in clubs and pubs and in performers like Ken Dodd, in my view a master of the art.

126. The End of the Music Hall Era (*Right*) the audience on the
last night of the Canterbury, May 1912.

"Thanks for the memory
I hope I've brought to you
More than a smile or two
I fear it's time to go now
Say 'tat tah' and 'toodle oo'
And thank you so much".

Roy Hudd, Cesars Palace Luton, 1975.